Wisdom

Violet

Sahasrara

Connection to the divine

Divine wisdom

Peaceful

Halo

White

Spiritual enlightenment

Harmony

Crown

Higher self

Unity

Bliss

Crown Chakra Adventures:

Exploring Wisdom
with
Amethyst and Violet

Volume 7

By: K.C Gold

"This book is dedicated to you.
Imagine a world beyond your wildest dreams."

Northern Lights Publishing LLC.

https://northernlightskids.com/

Hello, I'm Amethyst,
And Violet's my friend,
We are spinning energy particles
Where wisdom's journey begins.

We're found swirling around
The top of your head,
Our purple hue shining,
Where your spirit is led.

We are called the Crown Chakra,
Where spirit takes its flight,
A place of unity and oneness,
Shining with pure light.

We're the energy force that drives
Your spiritual connection,
A radiant stream of wisdom,
Higher consciousness in reflection.

We love to have fun
And assist you too,
But sometimes we need a
hand,
Just from you.

If you ever feel emptiness,

It means we're unbalanced,
Our spin's losing its height.

But don't you fret, for
solutions are in view,
To get us spinning back to
963 times plus two.

Hertz Meter

1 Hertz (Hz) = 1 Spin Per Second

963Hz

We love to hear pitch 'B',
Every time we hear that note,
We start to sway and swirl around
And even start to float.

Dance and move your head,
Now we're spinning around,
In a vibrant whirl of energy,
Where wisdom is found.

Eat something purple, a grape so sweet,
Nourishing your spirit with nature's gentle treat.

Dress in our color,
Violet looks good on you,
Radiating harmony, in all
that you do.

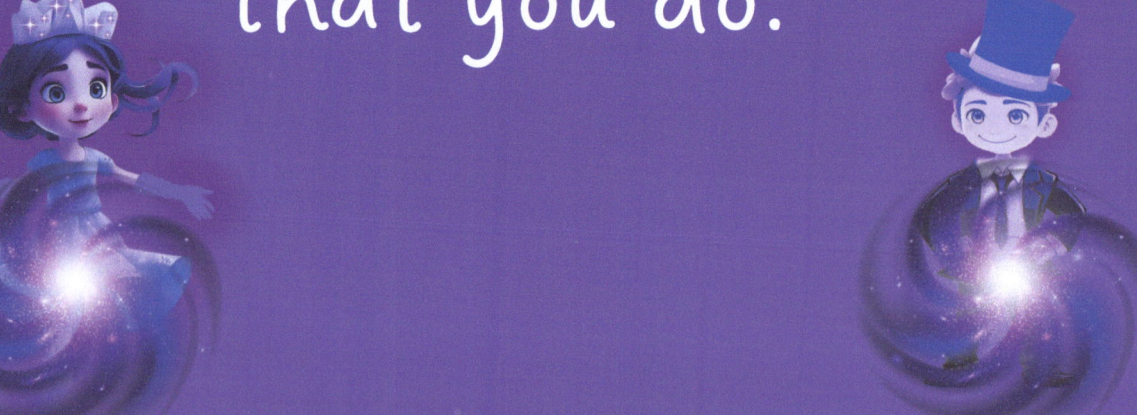

Close your eyes and let us
lead the way,
As we dance in the cosmos,
let your spirit sway.

Do whatever you need, we're
here for you,
Helping with your journey, in
all that you choose.

Sit in a quiet place, when you find the time, Repeat your favorite mantra, until you feel sublime.

"Connected to all,
near and far,
Shining brightly like a
twinkling star."

"Protected and inspired by the divine's design, In its love, forever I shine."

"In the universe's
embrace,
I find my place."

"Love and light, like a celestial shower,
Rain down on me, every single hour."

With wonder and wisdom, let your spirit soar high, Crown Chakra's guides you across the sky.

Wisdom
Violet
Sahasrara
Connection to the divine
Divine wisdom
Peaceful
Halo

Dear Reader,

Thank you for taking the time to read this book. If you found value in it, I would be incredibly grateful if you could take a few moments to leave a review. Your feedback not only helps me improve but also aids other readers in discovering books they might enjoy.

Thank you once again for your support and for being a part of this adventure!

Warm regards,
K.C. Gold

Amazon

Northern Lights
Publishing

Imagine a world beyond your wildest dreams.